RudderLess

The Loss of Leadership and Logic

For the Next Generation of Patriots

Jon A. DelVecchio

In every field of inquiry, it is true that all things should be made as simple as possible – but no simpler.

And for every problem that is muddled by over-complexity, a dozen are muddled by over-simplifying.

(Attributed to Albert Einstein in several publications 1964, 1972, et al.)

****

"You people are never going to remember this, you have to understand it!"

(Paraphrased by RIT Professor Biehler, in an applied science class, late 1960s)

V1

ISBN-13: 978-0692182192
ISBN-10: 0692182195

Library of Congress Control Number:
2018910961

Acknowledgements

The ideas contained in this book came from innumerable places collected over decades from all sorts of people. The collection of ideas came as a result of a lifetime full of a diverse set of events and interactions. Over the last few years I documented the observations presented in this book. I have to recognize nearly all my family and friends for active and passive listening, multiple news and information sources, and myself for documenting so I had something to actually publish. Special acknowledgement to Linda, my wife of 51 years, who often reminds me to "do something" about the state of affairs and my son, Jon J, who empowered me by his example and inspired me by beating me to the ranks of the published with his own successful book.

Biography

It's a good idea to know your sources, regarding this book, it's me. Information you receive gets filed away in your mind and you never know when it will be recalled. That's one reason why it is important to evaluate the source of information and probably why there are rules governing written copy. Early computer geeks had a term in computer data called "garbage in-garbage out". I would apply the GIGO concept to written copy relative to one's brain.

I am a family man with a wife of many talents and three adult offspring who have families and professional careers of their own. We have five grandchildren, all on career paths as well. I couldn't feel more fortunate or be more proud of the whole gang. Our gatherings are many and chaotic love fests, all with coffee and ridiculous amounts of food. Opinions on all sorts of things vary, sometimes passionately.

I have taken the opportunity and made the effort to be formally educated (engineering and business degrees) and professionally certified (New York State Professional Engineer and Project Management). Now retired, my 50 year working career spanned several private companies where I applied my formal knowledge and gained a wealth of experience, all shaping the opinions and positions in this book.

I regularly watch a spectrum of news, play at golf, strum guitar and fix things.

Full disclosure: I have innate sarcasm, a fixation on logic and results, am broadly curious and frustratingly optimistic. I have low tolerance for people who repeatedly say and do stupid things, especially when I know they know better.

Table of Contents

Prologue

Remember when society's leaders were valued? When they inspired others by "pointing the way" to common goals? When they spoke, people would listen and focus on those common goals?... So much for nostalgia.

To jog the memories of those who lived it and for historical knowledge for those who didn't, I believe a movement started, as most things do, with a bright side and an unintended dark side. The Vietnam War and ensuing social unrest was largely responsible for initiating a societal shift. Communications, especially visual communications, had become of age showing the tragedy of war and young Americans were being drafted (some would say "forced") to fight and die on foreign soil with seemingly unclear goals. US leaders "spun" the information as to "progress" in the war. As the spinning became uncovered, the seeds of distrust in leaders of all types, were planted. Distrust led to disrespect for just about anyone in a lead role. Fast forward to 2016. The pendulum has devolved to bizarre, irrational and violent behavior by large sectors of society against other sectors. This is exacerbated by media who have largely become conduits for chaos, assumedly for sensationalism, leading to "eyeballs", leading further to financial gain. The 4th estate duties of the media as the watchdog of government have long since been abandoned for profit and power. Ideological intolerance is rampant on the Left. The Right is developing an intolerance of its own. Growing sentiment on the part of "We the People" is to eliminate the extreme Left actions of violence, shout-down of free speech and disrespect for people who are taking action to improve lives of Americans. In short, the Right is through being "punished" for doing good deeds. This is especially true for President Trump.

Since 2016 election, now about 2 years ago, Left Leaners (LL) have gone crazy, becoming unable to discuss social issues rationally. Oft expressed hate for President Trump and his Right Leaning policies is widely displayed even to the point of denying free speech, challenging presumption of innocence and taking ridiculous positions. College Campuses have become bastions of socialism and political correctness with the additional ingredients of historical ignorance and violence against persons and property. University staff and administration freely allow extreme harassment against conservative people, violent protesting and denying speakers on campus with whom they disagree.

Media outlet reporting headlines the most negative parts of any action by the Trump Administration largely ignoring anything beneficial. (90+% negative reporting on Trump admin). This has reached the point where even elected officials openly defy Federal law, openly oppose peacemaking foreign policy by supporting US enemies, excuse violent gang activity and push for open borders.

College Campus Craziness is shown daily on FOX News but virtually buried on any other Media. A bright spot, Turning Point USA has arisen as an organization exposing universities harboring extreme leftist ideologies and propagandizing idealistic and ignorant students. TPUSA has progressed to a mainstream entity.

Open disdain and disrespect for law enforcement and common social decorum of any kind has grown to epic proportions. This is exacerbated by elected officials and media, as well. Policing is criticized for actually protecting and serving while criminal actors are touted as "expressing their rights".

The reversal and backward movement of what used to be norms caused me to begin writing down observations. Social and political ideological discussions inevitably led to widening division, especially with those on the ideological left. Respectful debating has been all but lost, even in public service where it is their elected duty to reach consensus. I expected that there would be disagreement by those whose candidate lost an election but I never expected the social division to reach such proportions or see its ability to last in public space as long as it has. I also never expected to see such acceptance to this divisive condition so harmful to peace, freedom, prosperity and societal development.

INSTRUCTIONS FOR READING

I admit to adopting a format that has been invented and used by many writers from Confucius' to modern times. The format is such that there is a page or two on most subjects. These are listed in the index and can be read in any order. The idea is that readers are supposed to do some thinking about the concepts and fit them in to their own lives.

I did this because my most memorable book on the subject of management was structured in this very practical way. The actual book was the 1st edition of "Up the Organization" by Robert Townsend, which was later updated with a bit of political correctness I suspect was mostly to sell more books to a later, more PC society. Townsend, I think, would rather have republished the 1st edition, since it was more direct. The reader has to look a bit harder for conceptual meaning in the 2nd edition, but the information is there.

Full disclosure is that I am pretty much in the middle of the road politically but firmly attached to results. When dealing with nearly any political (or any) problem, fully assess the parameters, look for historical precedent, do what is the most likely to work within the boundaries of the founder's constitutional vision, then clinically measure outcomes and adjust quickly to improve performance. Oh and most importantly, fixate on the goal and go for the win-win whenever you can.

One more thing. In the interest of "grounding" and "simplicity", you may want to first jump to the "APPLIED EPILOGUE" at the end of this book to test your knowledge of the concepts there.

1. Rational Discourse

Building throughout the 2016 Presidential election season, division between Right Leaners and Left Leaners continues to grow and morph into irrationality. Left Leaners can't seem to focus on rational debate. Anything Donald Trump does or says is immediately met with negative reporting by a large sector of the MAIN STREAM MEDIA and vile, even seditious commentary by Hollywood, Entertainers, Congressional members and others with influence. Left Leaners in general have lost any ability to view Donald Trump and anything he does as positive. If Donald Trump were shown walking on water, many would say, "look, Donald Trump can't swim!" They won't accept Donald Trump as POTUS or even acknowledge obvious improvement actions, which have been many, dwarfing any POTUS in recent history. This divisive environment, stubbornly focused on negatives, is crippling the effort to solve problems.

2. Ignorance

From the “man on the street” to news anchors there is a distinct lack of knowledge about the US as a republic, the free market, civic affairs and the unequalled benefit of living in the US as compared to anywhere else. I suspect it is largely not because the ignorant do not understand but that they will not understand. The problem with this is that ignorant arguments convince many people who can’t think critically. So called, famous people, tell the unknowing what they want to hear. It doesn’t have to be the truth for people to believe it, because they want to. This gets worse. People want to sound intelligent but when they realize that they can’t support their argument, they try to conserve their self-esteem by shouting down their “opponent” or by labeling the other person as a social outcast (i.e. racist, misogynist, fascist, etc.). In the end, there are too many people who have no business expressing their opinion because they spew untruths and omit pertinent facts. The MAIN STREAM MEDIA doesn’t help. They don’t expose these weak arguments and worse yet, fail to bring up salient questions of their own.

3. Political Correctness (PC)

PC culture started out innocently enough but looking back, had all the earmarks of doing more harm than good. Worse yet, it has spread to nearly every area of endeavor. The premise was weak to begin with and particularly dishonest. PC has led to more discrimination and elements of fascism affecting even those it was meant to "protect". PC causes more division, less tolerance and heightened feelings of being offended by, so called, protected individuals. This has further morphed into safe space demands, twisted support for illegal immigrants over American citizens, and violent actions by those who have been categorized by the PC culture as victims. Disdain for the protected classes (PCs) is now pervasive but largely underground because PCs have been given advantage over so called advantaged classes (ACs). Negative opinion of the PCs continues for several reasons because of the negative effect of PC culture. This has happened because ACs have been passed over for jobs, disciplined because of something they have said, had the bar lowered for hiring PCs over ACs, see entitlements grow wildly for PCs that ACs are paying for, are labeled (racist, misogynist, homophobic, xenophobic, etc.) for challenging liberal issues in any way. This keeps growing because there appears to be no stopping to the demands of the PCs. Society just can't give the PCs enough, reaching the point of absurdity. Building takeover by students demanding a segregated building for housing black students only and then further demanding a painting be hung honoring another country, disrespectful protests causing denial of Right Leaners events and speakers, MAIN STREAM MEDIA publishing unproven and damaging innuendos against individuals thereby violating their freedoms and safe pursuit of happiness. The extreme hypocrisy by the Left Leaners is largely evident in the treatment of POTUS. There is such negative and untruthful name calling and publications against the POTUS by exactly those who supposedly promote treating everyone with respect. A growing number of Americans are tiring of the leftist policies and PC culture. This is further demonstrated by Orwellian terms like "undocumented immigrants" instead of “illegal aliens” … or the latest in Seattle “community members” instead of “suspects”, “students” instead of “criminal inmates”. The pendulum appears to be swinging to the Right, and no one knows how far it will go.

4. Human Nature

There are certain innate proclivities in humans, such as security, social interaction, sexual preferences, food/shelter preferences, selfishness, etc. When laws or policies are made that conflict with these proclivities, trouble ensues. Anyone with even the most cursory understanding of social science knows that humans tend to be discriminating in the choices they make, say, for food, environmental comfort, people they associate with and life in general. In a free society like the US, personal choices can be termed as "rights", so long as the "rights" of others are protected. This takes discipline with the knowledge that most things are not just about you.

Our legislators are duty bound to apply the US Constitution as they produce legislation. Laws and policies that conflict with human nature need to consider that in our constitutional republic, citizens can't be forced to subdue their innate thoughts or actions. Our leaders tend to forget this and wrongly insert their own innateness into their positions, establishing governing laws resulting in conflict with natural law. They do this because they are "re-election" motivated instead of "governing" motivated. Human nature alone should be enough to make the case for term limits, without them, priorities get fuzzy.

With a knowledge of history and more than a few decades under my belt, my observation is that quality of products and services are trending downward for elected officials, school performance, consumer products, information, just to mention a few. To whom do we owe this condition?

I recall a cartoon with the final frame stating: "I found the problem and it's us".
We band together in our own groups and fight other groups. We tolerate failure by re-electing people who don't do their duty. Too many of us are information deprived despite the high development of communication technology. We cave to our innate instincts instead of leading disciplined lives that will result in a better future.

5. Illegal Immigration

To say the least, the US government has been lax in its enforcement of existing immigration law for decades. Because these laws have be poorly enforced for so long, illegal immigrants have been allowed to stay in the US, taking any resource or benefit they could legally or illegally acquire, and generally building a life and family ties as a US citizen would. So given the fact that poor enforcement of immigration law has been perpetuated for so long, there is a population of people who have grown roots who have not been naturalized and have refused assimilation, both requirements for reasonable immigration control and social order. Think of it as an equivalent to public domain ownership of copyrighted material. If you don't act to protect borders and citizenship, it becomes a sort of "right", simply because it wasn't protected. The good thing is that unlike "public domain claims" better enforcement can be done anytime the government decides to enforce. There are people who gain and people who lose in this environment. It is simply unfair and sometimes dangerous to American citizens. Illegal immigrants perform illegal acts at triple the rate of citizens (3.5% of population with 13% of crimes beyond the border crossing). There are also related negative consequences of lax border control including drug & human trafficking, smuggling of illegal drugs, increased risk of criminal activity, national security, etc. It is total nonsense and unpatriotic to continue to accept the current state of immigration enforcement. There have been perfectly reasonable approaches to immigration reform (Senator Rubio's & President Trump's plan) that can't even get non-partisan debate in Congress. After years of observation, I can say unequivocally that the left has not only blocked any progress on the problem but has made it worse by establishing DACA only for BHO's personal legacy which has shrunken to non-existence. Furthermore, anyone who blocks or slows progress on immigration reform or enforcement is misrepresenting their constituents at least and are committing treason at worst. Citizens don't report on criminal activity committed by community members, why should illegals report on their brethren? The courts need to enforce current law and stop playing politics with this issue, if not, judges should be impeached and removed from the bench. Similarly with those who rejected President Trump's extremely liberal immigration proposal in early 2018. Left leaning elected officials continue to fail and obstruct on this issue. They should be removed from office and replaced by those who will do their duty to produce effective immigration policies.

6. Release of Convicted Criminals

The early release of convicted felons has far reaching consequences. At the center of each case is a person who was lawfully imprisoned because of a felonious act. It is likely that a felon has had a lifetime of criminal activity. There may be compelling reasons why a person would choose to continue with such a life but the fact remains that the crimes are serious and the public needs protection from these individuals. We all know that there are disproportionate numbers of blacks in federal prisons, but the facts remain that they did the crime and have received sentences that are significantly less than statutory limits due to acceptance of lesser pleas. Worse yet the victim's justice is compromised and the recidivism rate is very high among released felons which cost even more to secure justice yet again and more victims are produced. Again We the People get hosed. Special interests are being served at the expense of the general public. Police become demoralized, more crime ensues, resulting in a destructive crime spiral. Personally, I am always disgusted to see a defendant, dressed neatly in an orderly court as a result of committing a heinous crime he obviously committed and soon to be incarcerated probably for less time and then cared for in a facility I have to pay for as a taxpayer. Not to mention that the inmates control way too much of the prison activities. How did that become acceptable? Improving general education and economic opportunities are great, but statistics show former convicts simply won't take advantage of the opportunity to turn their lives around. Intervention has to happen much earlier in life.

7. Legalization of Cannabis

Legalization of marijuana brings to mind a familiar scene. The family children insist on having a puppy. They promise to take care of the dog as it would be not only enjoyable to have a puppy but it would be a learning experience and somewhat therapeutic as well. Of course, the result most often is quite different. Mom or Dad winds up feeding, picking up waste, transporting to the vet, exercising, and establishing a close relationship with the dog. The kids, not so much. Reality bites.

Is cannabis legalization really so different? cannabis users push for legal use and have started a trend toward legalization stating medical use, conflicting "proof" of cannabis as not being a gateway drug and basic freedom of choice. So what really happens? It starts with "medicinal" use (the puppy), then eventually becomes broadly accessible. A whole new business develops. People get jobs from farmers to processors to retail clerks. A new form of social culture comes about. A windfall of tax revenue arises. Police workload is reduced. All is well and good until in a short time abuse becomes a social problem with more car accidents, more addicts committing crimes to fund their habit, minors obtain and get hooked on cannabis, illegal drug use becomes more prevalent, increased tax revenue is consumed by the need to enforce regulations, more court cases, more property damage increasing insurance rates for all, more rehab centers, dumbing down of young users' motivation to contribute to society, upward mobility is diminished.

In short, more people are free to become irresponsible and the rest of us pay by having to live in a downgraded environment and carry the burden of support. Worse yet, the addict never contributes to society and becomes just another wasted life. Reality bites.

8. Gang Violence

Finally, the Fed, under Trump, is taking action to go after the Urban Gangs, MS-13 specifically, probably others. It is about time. These gangs have existed with relative impunity. Killing, drug pushing, wrecking young lives. What is disturbing is that gang violence is not new. Urban centers have suffered this plague for decades and progressive policies have only worsened the situation. Immigration enforcement policies, political correctness, poverty, and anti-cop attitudes have exacerbated the violence. Fear prevents victims and community people from cooperating with police to rid themselves of the scourge. Our urban neighbors are essentially living in an autocratic state. Elected officials don't appear to care that life in urban communities is totalitarian and limits the urban community's pursuit of happiness. Instead young people join the thugs in order to survive. This virtually stops traditional, law abiding development, only adding to the scourge. Local Police need to be unchained with eliminating the gangs and to work in cooperation with Federal Authorities. Arrest and incarceration are only treating the symptom, ineffectively, I might add.

Somehow the cycle has to be broken. The so called, "progressives" continue to come up with faux actions to break the cycle, but they haven't worked. Even Elvis Presley's song "In the Ghetto" exposed the problems in the urban culture, 50 years ago.

The fix isn't rocket science, it is way more difficult. It is an established cycle promulgated by known human behavior at its very basic level. Maslow's hierarchy of human needs easily characterizes the urban culture problems as physiological and safety from harm. In simple terms, until a person is safely housed and fed, he or she cannot even consider the upward mobility through the hierarchy.

Urban Chaos has to be assessed in a clinical and not a political manner. The Urban population needs to take some responsibility in this effort. For whatever reason the Urban poor can't or won't help to break the grip of crime and we have to stop the spread of gang crime. Any ideas, progressives? I'm all ears.

9. Guns

There are simply too many guns accessed by bad actors and mentally ill people. Increasing education and restrictions on law abiding gun owners are likely have minimal impact compared to an effort to keep guns away from dangerous people. Division over improving regulation is distracting from real improvement. While gun control arguments continue, background checks, illegal gun trafficking and mental illness actions are held up. There have been reports and even documentaries on gun running. I would bet there are many people, including law enforcement, who see and know about crimes associated with the gun running logistics, illegal gun ownership and how to identify illegal guns being carried on the street. Politicizing this issue is simply public servants not doing their job.

10. Free Speech

The first amendment is suffering an assault as never seen before. Conservative or traditional views on all sort of issues are being "censored by the mob". This could also be defined as anarchy, fascism and lawlessness. This "mobocracy" cannot be tolerated and must be squashed immediately wherever it arises. These are criminal acts on public and private property and should be prosecuted. This appears as violent demonstrations, media attacks, professorial threatening, politically correct word control, "safe space" rules, heckling, etc. In short, everyone has the right to speak, even so called "hate speech" is protected. This is the law of the land and must be protected at all costs. It is at the root of who we are as a nation. Social media (FB, TWTR, GOOGLE, etc) is at the heart of the speech control by using their so called "algorithms" that search for and block speech, hiding behind PC offensive phrases. The Truth is, and there is plenty of supporting evidence, that speech is blocked on social media by progressive minded algorithm writers that he or she doesn't like or is offended by. They should be fired.

From the Freedom Forum, there are basically nine categories of unprotected speech:

- Obscenity
- Fighting words
- Defamation (including libel and slander)
- Child pornography
- Perjury
- Blackmail
- Incitement to imminent lawless action
- True threats
- Solicitations to commit crimes
- Plagiarism
- Verbally committed Treason

That's it folks!

11. Ideological Equivalency (or Lack of)

When lies or deceit by media or politicians is observed, people often claim "well, they (politicians & government officials) all do it". First off, there is no equivalency. The Right acts quite differently from the Left. Generally, people on the Right, even far Right, will listen to and give common respect to the left. Not so with the reverse. Left leaners tend to shout down, interrupt, make disparaging statements, make incomplete assessments on issues, rarely come up with potential solutions and when that fails, use violence and riot to get their way. The proof? One has to only observe the chaos on college campuses, mob threats on private property (restaurants, residences) and anti-police demonstrations.

12. Profiling

Profiling has been twisted by the PC culture to be the major cause of unrest, especially among urban communities. People have been propagandized by the Left that they are victims of profiling. Profiling is an innate function of humans. We do it all the time. It is part of human survival instinct. It is further refined in law enforcement training to be used as a tool in determining probability of criminal activity or personal injury. It has also been largely locked up in the law enforcement toolbox due to progressive policy and disciplinary action against police officers who use profiling tactics they have been taught. The practical matter is, police department policy can deny "profiling" but they cannot stop officers from the very instincts they were born with. Furthermore, profiling has been very effective in police work, proven by stop and frisk activity. No one likes being searched and it doesn't help police-community relations but considering the negative results (deaths) of illegal gun possession, profiling policies and para-military practices should be unleashed in known trouble spots, denying safe haven for bad actors. We all know that criminals take advantage of the anti-profiling stance by "progressive policing" and the fear of law abiding residents.

13. Motivation

When presented with general comments, policy positions, or candidates for political office, I first consider what their motivation might be. I try to determine this so I can place context into statements and also to give a modicum of respect to opposing views.

Seeking one's motivation is telling in many social situations. Consider for a moment Donald Trump. What is his motivation? Why would a fabulously rich person like Mr. Trump want to be the president? He is extremely comfortable financially. He appears vigorous and healthy, has a beautiful family, travels at will anywhere in the world in his own luxurious airplane, and seems to enjoy his 70 year old life immensely. He needs no more money or fame so it might just be that he wants to make badly needed improvements in the lives of many of his fellow citizens. Is he perfect? No one is. Will he and his family gain by helping others gain wealth? Of course. Does he have the skills to manage the largest service organization in the world? I am challenged to name anyone better, even after only a few months in office.

Consider using the motivation assessment technique. Apply it to everyday personal interactions, and I believe you will gain insight as to “where a person is coming from”. Political ideology is a glaring example. Aren’t you a little bit curious as to why seemingly intelligent, rational people you know are so divided on politics to the point of disrespecting others, screaming tirades and blind ignorance on civics? Motivational assessment does not take a degree in psychology. We are all born with the ability to assess the motivation of another person. How?... because they’ll tell you, if they know themselves, that is.

I held up the completion of this book in order to modify my previous version of Motivation. This delay came as a result of observing the Judge Kavanaugh--Supreme Court hearings. We all know that the Left wants an activist Supreme Court. We know the Democrats on the Judicial Committee know what presumed innocence is.

I have to ask myself why Senators on the Left are rationalizing against the "presumption of innocence", a pillar of our judicial system. I have the answer. Motivation.

The Democrat Senators' goal is staying in power, not serve their constituents. The media is looking for "eyeballs" leading to higher revenues, not balanced reporting. Finally, our lefty friends, family and neighbors identify so strongly with their political ideology that they toss off common decency and simple logic. It doesn't take a doctorate in psychology to see that Right Leaners are constantly being disrespected, called despicable names, falsely accused of the most heinous acts, wrongly associated with criminals and criticized for their ideological positions. Anyone can see that there is no moral equivalence regarding actions of the Right and Left. It is glaringly obvious that the Right thinks the Left is WRONG and the Left thinks the Right is EVIL and the Left will do anything, including despicable & unpatriotic acts, to support their selfishness.

Lastly, I'll say that Left Leaning Citizens have aligned themselves solely with their ideological positions. It is, in their mind, who they are. They just don't get the idea that it is "We the People" who are not being served by politicians and the 4th estate media watchdogs. It is these entities that are not serving but dividing us in order to serve their own ambitions and wealth. In short, their Motivation is in conflict with their respective duties. It's us in conflict with the media and elected officials, so stop blaming fellow citizens. The establishments work for "We the People", not the other way around.

14. Competency

Individual and organizational competency seems to be at an all-time low. In the 80s there was an enormous movement for continuous quality improvement. This movement has all but disappeared and worse yet, we as receivers of goods and services seem to willingly accept it. I try not to get angry over it but it has become a pet peeve of mine. Service performance is especially decaying. This is obviously seen in the VA, law enforcement tolerance of urban violence and repetitive failure of our elected officials. It appears nearly everywhere from cooking a cheeseburger to health care. It seems the drive for quality performance is non-existent. There is no shortage of superlative claims by promotional messaging, but it seems we as consumers accept mistakes, inaccuracy and poor service as a matter of course. Whatever happened to pride in our work, to truly doing our best, to clear goal orientation, to effective management? People always say they want the best surgeon, or top tradesman or the best performing equipment but it seems we as a society have come to accept “good enough” instead of “good”. Bringing “value” into decisions we make is a good thing, but very often no real comprehensive comparison is done. “Caveat emptor” is all but gone as well. Actually, this is relatively simple to fix. We all need to fairly enforce accountability. Management sets goals, workers focus on those goals. We the People are the “Management” when it comes to governance. We need to hold accountable (Goods & Services failures) managers and vote out “government employees” who don’t perform.

15. Education

Even in a dumbed down school environment, there are less than 50% graduation rates in cities. (Those who started 9th grade and graduated together, assumedly 4 years later). Reading and Math proficiency (Niche.com) in the Rochester NY City School District is at 16% and 18% in 2016, respectively. This is deplorable and it isn't because of lack of funding. Generally, this journalistic sourced statement can summarize New York State's performance. *"While New York spends $24 billion a year on its schools — by far the most in the nation — taxpayers get middling results in return."* This dismal performance is a result of multiple factors from political appointees on the state board, to poor performing school administrations, to poor parenting, to tolerance for negative behavior, to economic dependency and generally lack of motivation to excel. Why aren't parents hopping mad and protesting to the school boards, holding them accountable? Maybe they don't want to accept that parents are a major part the problem through ignorance, poor parenting practices, selfishness, dependency on others, single motherhood-vacant fatherhood?

Beyond the parents or the schools themselves, what is the reason that societies fund and support education. It is of course to educate the next generations so they can sustain the society long term. Failure to effectively educate children in the long view leads to demise of that society. We cannot leave our children with a declining environment, it is simply irresponsible.

16. Lies

Lies are one of the words in the English language that has lost its true meaning. There are others (discrimination, "isms", facts, etc.). Weasel words referring to lies like...untruths, half-truths, white lies, incorrect statements, unsubstantiated "facts" or wrongly applied meanings...only serve to confuse the issue at hand, which then causes communication effectiveness to suffer, eventually inhibiting the valid purpose of the communication. This is particularly damaging when serious issues such as safety, security, life and illness are the subject of the communication. The major problem with this is that there is confusion created by the misuse and inherent misunderstanding caused by the use of misleadingly applied words. Different individuals use dramatically applied words interchangeably, either to purposefully control a narrative or that simply use the wrong description. The liberal or indiscriminate use of these words only serves to slow positive discussion or action and also taints individual trust and credibility ("people will die,

Armageddon, crumbs, hate speech") . The only way to defeat this is to clarify while rationally communicating. It gets tiresome to have to explain the meaning of words you use while one is expressing a thought. More time and effort needs to be spent in order to have debate on any subject. Anger, frustration, hate and violence have no part to play in problem solving.

A consequence of the use of misapplied words referring to "lies" is that one is never sure of the true meaning. There is no downside to what is really a lie. It is generally accepted by the Right that Obama lied about keeping your doctor and your med plan and reduced costs when he promoted ACA. If Obama had simply corrected this statement as ACA was finally proposed for congressional approval, there wouldn't have been good reason to claim this as a lie. What turned it into a lie was having context with other statements regarding ACA. Like stating that ACA was really a tax, or that there would be a reduction in HC cost to all, or that it would provide better HC. This simply did not happen, so more misleading continues to occur. Real people suffer with a still an unknown Federal health care policy after 8 years of ACA. There have been no consequences for causing the poorest among us being forced to suffer illness without care, or having to pay ever increasing insurance coverage costs. Individuals and businesses are paying high costs for coverage or simply paying "tax" not to have insurance. Parts of the ACA are simply proven by SCOTUS to be unconstitutional.

At this point, we could discuss lies and misleading statements since ACA has been law for eight years. This lag from promise to proof causes yet another negative consequence. No one is held accountable for these lies. Once enough time passes and more issues come up, the general public and politicos are on to the next shiny object, there by accepting the lies by default. The most devious among us take advantage of this delay in accountability. This advantage appears in investigation boondoggles, denials, old news, missing data, missing people, and 5th amendment claims. When current authority tries to exercise accountability, they are ignored and inhibited by opposing politicians, media and even the person who is the subject of the investigation. In the end, We the People lose. Few are held accountable for obvious lies.

17. Fascism

This is another misuse of a word used to shock or wrongly categorize people and ideology. One can only assume that this is done to further an ideological agenda. Fascism by definition is *(in general use) extreme right-wing, authoritarian, or intolerant views or practice*. The word also conjures up Nazi Germany and Hitler, universally hated but also useful in disadvantaging political opponents during debate. This tactic is used by a number of Left Leaners even when they themselves are committing Fascist acts. Shout downs, physically attacking ideological opponents, violent demonstrations, all kinds of anti-police activity, are commonly used by extreme Left Leaners and not condemned by more moderate Left Leaners, who appear to accept this criminal behavior. Not so with even with the most extreme Right Leaners. Once the word fascist or terrorist is attached, rational conversation is over.

A prime source for Fascism is "antifa". This group describes themselves as anti-fascists.

Nothing could be further from the truth. Their actions have Fascism written all over them. This group, (antifa) is nothing but a group of misguided thugs aiming to violently attack peaceful protest and free speech.

18. Respect

In a social sense, common respect has seriously decayed. Disagreement has become absolute. Debate, even on minor issues, has morphed into dramatic, violent argument. Worse yet when political ideology is the subject, things turn ugly very quickly. Recently, a college professor was video recorded while physically attacking an opposing protestor holding a sign. As she pounded her relatively small fists against the sign holder, he ignored her until she was assisted by one of her supporters in knocking the opposing sign holder to the ground, who was then further mob attacked after falling to the ground by punching, kicking and stomping. She was interviewed by Tucker Carlson who showed the offending video. This professor actually claimed that if anyone supported President Trump or spoke against her ideology, that she was within her rights to stop free speech expression, physically if necessary. This professor was later charged and convicted of assault. Any American with any understanding of US law, policy and/or legacy should see this as anarchy and support the removal of this person from teaching. Yet these ideological acts are often glossed over by MAIN STREAM MEDIA or not even reported. One can only assume that MAIN STREAM MEDIA and Left Leaners support the trend to destroy free speech while practicing violent authoritarianism.

19. Power to Influence

We the People need to do our individual part to hold elected officials accountable. We have more tools than ever, beyond the voting booth, including email, town halls, texting, Twitter, internet article comments, or handwritten letters. It has never been easier to let our opinions be known to those in power. As individuals we also need to push back against opposing opinions. Some of these actions take little effort to be effective. The time has passed when the silent majority can stay silent. We the People must let our opinions be known. Special interest groups have been very successful in getting their ideologies ingrained in our everyday lives to the point of ridiculousness. PC culture, light sentencing, pardons/early release of criminals, illegal immigrant acceptance, urban culture acceptance, hog tying police, acceptance of government incompetence, overblown entitlements at every level of government, late term abortions, frivolous lawsuits, activism in conflict with law abiding citizen's safety and freedoms. Left Leaning citizens are lambs to slaughter, led by Hollywood, Entertainers, and MAIN STREAM MEDIA who are driven by fame and profits. Americans need to avoid being influenced by ignorant, self-serving people and make an effort to avoid becoming one of them. P.T. Barnum had a phrase for this. "There is a Sucker born every minute".

Don't be a sucker.

20. Political Power

Political office was envisioned by the founding fathers as an obligatory service commitment to, and for, fellow citizens. Since then political office has become a career, carrying with it high respect, social power and wealth. It is obvious that holding political office is so beneficial to the office holder that getting elected greatly overshadows not only the service element of the position but brings out "flexible" integrity of officeholders as well. Politicians seem to forget those they represent until election time. Then, promises are made and routinely ignored after election. We the People have allowed this to happen. Politicians' actions appear only to support legislation in order to cater to special interests while deceiving others that believe election rhetoric. It has been suggested that Political Science be eliminated as study and career. Does anyone think that a lifetime on a government payroll was an intent of the Founders? A major change to term limits could have a corrective effect on the performance of our representatives. (Don't hold your breath)

Until then however, We the People, need to hold politicians accountable by paying attention and communicating often.

21. Decay of Parenting

I struggle with the issue of parenting. I don't know how this evolved exactly but how did the degradation of children's behavior get to such a point. I thought back to previous generations and realized that this degradation was more of an evolution than a point in time where it began. Certainly there were major incidents like the Kennedy assassination, the Vietnam War, the Watergate conspiracy, War on Poverty, etc. that caused the disrespect for any kind of authority from Government to Police, then further into the Courts, Congress, Corporations, Colleges and Parents themselves. Disrespect by students has even crept into Primary Schools.

Gen X parenting is especially telling. Their children are school age at this point and behavioral data is current. This is not to say that Gen X or their children are to "blame" or that all Gen X families are the same but they represent the current student environment.

We “Baby Boomers” (BBs) seemed to have taken the first turn toward a disrespecting attitude. This is not to say that this attitude is unwarranted. There is plenty of support for BBs to have developed a distrust for the “establishment”. The divisive split however may have come about as BBs came into adulthood. Hippies, beatniks and peaceniks spent their early adult years protesting and engaging in chemical abuse. Yet another large part of the young adult population, worked their way toward more traditional work and family. Both groups had valid views on American life, where people could freely choose what they wanted their life to be. On the other hand, some life choices were not sustainable as the years passed, there needed to be a more flexible and continuous learning approach to life mostly due to accelerated technology and communication networking. Instead of accepting and working within an ever changing world, too many adults have either irrationally held on to traditional and/or idealistic values. The problem with this unhealthy attachment to the past or to “progressive” ideology is that it hurts the learning generation. It is simply not

OK to support or participate in this irrationality. Parents need to adopt the most effective methods and context, in order to pass traditional social values forward, resulting in a sustainable American future.

22. Illegal and Controlled Substances

A suggestion for solution.
There are valid points of view on both sides of the legalization of weed (pot or Cannabis if you prefer), or for that matter, any drug. On one side, freedom, medical use, new business growth, increased tax revenue and reduced cost of law enforcement. On the other side, marijuana is a proven gateway to harder illegal substances, user sloth and criminality, irresponsible access by children, increased traffic accidents, general impact on non-user cost and safety. So how can we reduce the negatives and maintain our freedoms. The answer seems simple… responsibility and accountability. The problem is too many in current US population have little appetite for accepting either responsibility or accountability. Users, in turn expose the rest of us to the negative results. In short, users get more freedom, non-users get less. So if there could be more responsibility and accountability on the part of users, legalization could work if regulated properly. This could be a compromise solution, not particularly the best

solution. It does however expand freedoms while allowing for progress on reducing the negatives. Eventually, users wouldn't be chosen for jobs or be attractive as spouses or parents, the smarter users would see the error of their ways and act responsibly; all with regulatory and rehabilitation support funded by the generated revenue.

It may be a long while, maybe never, that social culture will act in a corrective manner. Until then, in an attempt to get the trafficking of controlled substances under some semblance of "control", measures need to be taken to disrupt the illegal flow. Illegal drug users are generally irresponsible people who contribute little or nothing to society. It is in fact the exact opposite. Drug users drain medical resources in their feigned attempt to be rehabilitated. Clearly, dealers and users are costing the rest of society pain, anguish and consuming scarce resources. One partial solution could be to send users who repeatedly failed rehabilitation, to be separated in a manner that would keep them off the streets, away from the flow of drugs, cared for and mentored by professionals but contained by kind of a white collar incarceration facility where inmates would be assigned jobs that would defray the cost of the facility. Meanwhile, they could be learning a trade or skill that could be applied when released. The location needs to be far from inmates' home neighborhoods and visits by outsiders would be rare, if ever. Failure to rehabilitate during or after sentenced time, would result in prison incarceration, like three time felony inmates. The psychological concept here would be that if a drug user is made to understand that if he becomes a three time rehab failure, he ends up in prison. This would increase his motivation to rehabilitate and learn a job skill. Elements of this idea require adjustment but could continue in keeping with the goal of separation from drug traffic flow, improving opportunities for rehabilitated users and avoidance of physical harm to law abiding citizens caused by the drug trade. President Trump's "opioid" actions need to publish their goals and report often.

23. Disdain for Free Market Policies

FIRE! BAD! Picture this in prehistory. Grog starts a fire for the first time. Gring, having seen the devastating result of fire by lightning, runs off, terrified. Grog on the other hand using his meager intelligence feels the heat but thinks…. How can I use this "fire"? he thinks… Keeping the cave warm, protection from beasts, heating food, attracting mates, etc.

Gring eventually peers out from behind a rock and returns thinking.. "I like warmth and protection and food and mating, too", He realizes that fire can be good and bad. In short, the rewards outweigh the risks.

Is the establishment of the free market really so different? It has rewards and risks. Just like fire has a downside, a free market isn't a perfect economic system. Reasonable people can agree that the risks of someone becoming filthy rich, some unable to cope or compete, and some becoming downright greedy are far outweighed by many more people having opportunity for jobs, innovation, and whatever else that personal wealth can offer. No other economic system has ever been as effective for freedom and personal wealth. In addition, where the negatives have arisen, regulation has been applied, then generally overdone.

So why are the promoters, users and benefactors of the US free economy so vilified? Those who created and run businesses, also create jobs and support benefits for people who create their own paths to wealth. Furthermore, the wealthiest among us support organizations for any number of disadvantaged people. I would rather support the people and organizations that support my causes rather than have an ever expanding government bureaucratic agency decide where my money is spent. To a reasonable person, constant criticism and application of regulations is nonsense. Critics only bring up negatives. Many say that they have the right to criticize, but to what end? It is almost never done in an evolutionary way but almost always in a revolutionary way that would bring down the free market system without offering something better.

Assuming critics are rational, I wonder what their motivation is. Are they jealous? Do they crave power to influence? Is it their way to fame? …or is it just that they are irrational or completely ignorant on this subject. I don't know because I can't read their minds. I can see the results of their protesting and sometimes violent mob actions. These people are not helping. They are causing more sloth, degrading our social values and slowing down economic progress and the benefits of expanded wealth. To be sure, they are hurting the rational majority, the very people who make America what it is. Name any other country people are dying to get into.

24. The Courts

The courts, especially the Federal level courts, are lifetime appointments. This was established in the constitution so that the courts would be non-political and rule in concert with Constitutional law. Federal courts, especially at the Circuit level, have become political tools of the left. All one has to do is to read the explanation of the decisions written by the courts to see which are reading bias in their opinions.

Chief Justice Roberts writes in the SC decision regarding "Whiting" that...
"It should not be surprising that the two dissents have sharply different views on how to read the statute. That is the sort of thing that can happen when statutory analysis is so untethered from the text."

For us legal novices, "untethered" in this comment refers to a recent SC Justice Sotomayor opinion which indicates bias interpretation instead of Congress' and/or Founders' actual contextual intent. Bias has no place in the courts, they need a fair understanding and opinion of the law as stated. Grossly divergent opinions should be grounds for impeachment and removal of judges who consistently write these "untethered" opinions. We the People rely on Congress to clearly legislate and the Courts to follow the laws as written. We the People are generally not legal experts and need to keep an eye on our elected officials and lifetime appointed persons. We can do this by finding fair and balanced reporting. Sotomayor on "Whiting" and "Schuette" are two examples of untethered bias. The dissenting opinions, if adopted, would have caused more litigation, more confusion, more court cases & injunctions based on unconstitutionality… and the dissenting justices know it. We don't need this.

25. Criminal and Seditious Groups

Black Lives Matter, Urban Gangs, Illegal Alien supporters, radical IMAMs exemplify Sedition in US modern society. They are far beyond protest and should be prosecuted and stamped out. Radical IMAM rants have been suggested as likely influences on homegrown terrorists. Could the innocent deaths of 9/11 been avoided if the rants were reported or prosecuted as seditious? We will never know. In the US we have come to ignore this incendiary, illegal speech which goes on with impunity. Considering that the West is in a war with jihadists, this speech should be regarded as wartime treason and dealt with as such. It could also be applied to anyone who impedes the performance of I.C.E. and extreme vetting for those seeking asylum or residency in the US. Citizens are being harmed by these so called activists. When will the victims see justice and elected officials held accountable for their obstruction and inaction?

26. U.S. Economy

The Economy is the heart of the US. It has been said that "money isn't everything but it beats the heck out of whatever is in second place". It's great to adopt a non-materialistic lifestyle but in the end, most of us would rather have the means to make the most out of American life from good health to entertainment… and that requires money. Reality bites.

The economy is so important that there must be a single minded focus on improving the economy by our leaders. Except for national security, our elected officials should have the health of the economy on the top of their list of things to do every day. Once action on sustaining economic improvement is addressed for the day, then and only then should one move on to other priorities.

27. Populism/MAGA/America First

Government officials are elected to represent all law abiding Americans, not foreigners, not crooks, not special interests. Once We the People have been fully attended to and 100% of us have been properly protected, have jobs, are able to freely pursue opportunities and enjoy whatever religion they want, then our elected representatives can take their limited legislative time to consider legislating and executive ordering on behalf of foreigners, convicted felons and any other special interest groups. Legislative action by Congress must avoid overreaching basic constitutional responsibilities and avoid taking on issues better served by state or local government and individuals themselves. Long range planning for Health Care, Education and Trade come to mind where the Fed has some role to play, albeit limited. States want freedom to provide for their constituents but they must provide responsible government and limit reliance on the Federal government. Similarly, individuals need to contribute to society and take on responsibility for themselves and their families.

28. Violence and Terrorism

There is a growing acceptance or resolution regarding violence. Some say it is something we have to learn to live with. The concern is that if We the People accept the idea that every week or two, we will be subjected to mass killing and mayhem, it will only get worse. More killing, more criminals, more victims, more police work, more money spent on courts and prisons, more people not contributing to the general good.

Continuous effort must be made to fight the growing violence. Law abiding citizens should inform police and be protected, shielded from the perpetrators. This should include friends, family and acquaintances who observe criminal activity. Furthermore, any associates of perpetrators should be investigated as accomplices. This will allow Law Enforcement to more effectively act in a preemptive fashion. Further action should be taken to charge, or at least investigate, all associates of perpetrators. It is known that weapons trafficking is out of any sort of control. Law Enforcement should be tasked to track down the trafficking lanes and reinstitute stop and frisk, using effective profiling methods as necessary. National background checks and mental illness also need to be addressed. This is all aimed at protecting citizens, the prime purpose of government, especially the Fed.

29. Boomers (B), GenXers (G), Millenials (M)

Chronology has taken US population through the “Greatest Generation” and is now a composite of B, G and Ms. Maybe it has always been this way where older generations lack confidence in the succeeding generation being able to carry on with the overall societal progress of the US. There is generally no question that since 1900, each generation has progressed by nearly any measure. Despite the enormous gains in communications and wealth, the Gs, and more so the Ms, appear to take advantage of the knowledge and wealth gained by previous generations to further progress. The Gs and Ms enjoy the progress just fine, but as a group, don’t have the wherewithal to continue the progress made by previous generations. Boomers lack confidence in the Gs and much more so the Ms, regarding their inability to “stand on generational shoulders”. The information to continue progress is easily found but the ability to apply and enhance the knowledge or values developed over the last century appears to the Bs to be highly questionable. Witness the low High School graduation rates, unacceptable reading and math proficiencies, social media content, violent demonstrations against any authority and is demonstrated by every "opinion on the street" event. The move toward socialism by the Gs and Ms is truly alarming and is growing in the ranks of the galactically ignorant.

30. Code Speak

Some call it "dogwhistle", others call it "code", but whatever it's called, this concept is divisive and destructive to communication. It is so pervasive that it enters nearly every discourse. It confounds effective discussion. An example would be the term "extreme vetting" regarding immigration. Many stubbornly perceive this to mean xenophobia. So if one suggests extreme vetting when it comes to immigration, Left Leaners perceive the intention is only to deny Muslims access to safe haven when in fact extreme vetting is a multifaceted concept with the prime purpose of protecting Americans which is exactly what POTUS is elected to enforce. In the larger sense, effective discourse is hampered by Left Leaners perception of intention so debate is stopped. Left Leaners think they hear "dog whistles" when in fact they miss or won't even listen to the clearly stated intention of the Right Leaners debate points. In a sense, it is conspiratorial to approach debate with bias that wrongfully impugns one's debate opponents. Debates end with no offer of solutions, just bad feelings.

Left Leaners seem blind to the fact that they label Right Leaners as liars with evil intentions. I have had enough of this. What gives Left Leaners the psychic ability to know their debate opponents intentions? The phrase "dogwhistle" is a tipoff and codifying speech should be exposed every time it is observed.

31. Freedom

Freedom for all is the simple concept that could describe what the framers were aiming for. If our elected leaders were to consider how "freedom for all" and the "America First" concept was impacted when developing legislation, there would be fewer laws, lower cost of government and less opportunity for corruption. Elected officials' first and foremost job is to represent all Americans in their respective districts and make the tough decisions to give due attention to the majority of their voters. They should promote opportunities more and legislate handouts to needy people less. How hard is that? If the elected folks can't do this, voters should "fire" them, then replace them with representatives who can.

Freedom is everything.

32. Selfishness

A human trait from birth. Nothing is more selfish than a newborn. Human development is largely teaching children to respectfully and effectively interact with other people. As children approach school age, selfishness should be controlled to the point where interaction with non-family members becomes prevalent. Representatives at all levels of government should know they are there to serve and show leadership in that regard. Service is the complete opposite of selfishness, yet selfishness is in full display almost everywhere one looks. People in positions of power using their positions and platforms to promote themselves in terms of wealth and political power. This appears as the 4th Estate (MSM) sensationalizing and parsing issues that sell more papers or "eyeballs"; politicians deceitfully doing the same in order to stay in power; radical groups violently demonstrating; idealists who support organizations like antifa; Resistance, Black Lives Matter, NeoNazis, never Trumpers, elitist individuals etc., ….and NOT the US Constitution. All these protesting groups have at least one selfish thing in common, BLINDNESS regarding the impact of their protests on the rest of us. Only their positions are valid and anyone who disagrees with them is termed evil or ignorant, therefore justifying that other opinions be shouted down, libeled, physically harmed or property destroyed. This leads to even greater division, turmoil and lack of law and order. The number of law abiding, everyday citizens is growing and becoming more intolerant of this behavior. The danger is that division and violence will likely increase before it gets better. Individuals are challenged to critically assess the veracity of their own ideology and positions.

33. Critical Thinking

Virtually non-existent on the left. The assault on Critical Thinking is vast. Rabid Consumerism, Easy use of Technology, and Misguided Parenting/Leadership are chief among the assault. These concepts tend to reduce the personal responsibility and ambition of a large sector of society. That sector looks to others to make decisions, guidance on raising their families, and financially support by others. It seem they have adopted the alt-JFK challenge. “Demand what the country can do for you, and protest when it doesn’t.” Too many people can’t or won’t think for themselves. They won’t spend the time on details of an issue preferring instead to disparage others’ opinions, tap screens on smartphones and spew bumper sticker phrases. This sector is vulnerable to charlatans of all sorts who recognize this irresponsible attitude, leveraging it to sell products and ideologies. Worse yet, when people in this sector are challenged, they feel attacked, then stubbornly hold their ground to save face, many act out violently. Even more disturbing is that they infect their offspring with nonsense, causing downward spiral of ignorance.

34. Misplaced Tolerance

The rise in incompetency or ineffectiveness in the performance of one's duty is pervasive. This condition is often seen in everyday life. It ranges from a poorly cooked restaurant meal to careless disclosure of highly sensitive, classified information. What is worse however, is that this has become nearly commonplace with the casual acceptance by too many Americans. The failures are numerous including poor job training, ineffective supervision, careless/incompetent incumbents, short life products, watered down education standards, scamming of entitlements, passionate misunderstanding, misleading of facts relating to important societal issues and selfishness by those in authority. We, as customers, should not accept poor quality of product or performance. Individuals need to complain to the "management", those who have training, hire and fire power over the poor performers. When it comes to government, We the People are in the management role. Be a smart voter. Understand why you support any candidate and how they relate to the elected position.

35. Urban Culture

This term is meant to describe the evolution of societal norms diverting away from traditional American culture such as respect for and drive toward hard work as a means of pursuing happiness.

Comparing the formative environments of the "Boomer" population (B) with the "Millennial" (M) population will serve to describe the cultural shift. Also noted, the Gen X (X) population represents a sort of transition period. The B was raised by the Greatest Generation (G) who were raised by the Immigrant Generation (I). The I willingly, and at great risk, left their countries of origin to become Americans. The G were infused with patriotism as their parents found work and wealth in America. Depression struggles, war service and a period of economic rebirth further burnished the G as patriots who in turn were examples of American life to the B. The B developed through fairly prosperous times but generally held on to traditional American life exemplified by economic growth, education of youth, respect for authority and self-sustainment. As media, TV and education developed, early adult years for B began to erode the traditional American life. Leaders were held in less regard, desire to improve the lives for the less fortunate and political expediency led to major trends of social activism. Politicians follow trends very closely and in order to get votes, joined the trend. Intentions were good but many in the B failed to see unintentional consequences of the activist trend. The trend expanded into parenting, education and general social values, shaping the X. The trend was viewed as "progressive" where more freedom, lowered moral values, adoption of evolving technology, reduction of personal responsibility coupled with a need to "help" the less fortunate became a social norm. This led further to a weakening of personal upward mobility in the X while denigrating the more fortunate members. Still there was a significant number of those who largely held on to free market values but generally failed to instill these values in M. The M adopted burgeoning communication technology and were given credit for having tech knowledge because they could operate a computer or cell phone. The fact that M possessed little knowledge of American values of G or B went unnoticed, bolstered by conspicuous consumerism and coddling of M as children. This environment apparently led to various levels of guilt in the middle and upper classes causing an unhealthy need to share good fortune with the less fortunate. Unhealthy in the sense that B, X and M went to extremes of supporting programs aimed at improving the fortunes of the lower economic classes. This in turn caused dependence on those programs, reduction in upward mobility, motivation, low social expectations and even criminality. This has now reached epic proportions of societal divisiveness, acceptance of pervasive poor job performance, softening of negative consequences for anti-social behavior, and vilifying of those holding on to traditional American values while expecting them to financially and socially support the downward trends. Pessimistically, this could lead down the path of the historically documented, "life cycle of nations" (LCN). Optimistically, this could be cyclical, having to "burn itself out" before reversing the downward social trend. I tend to be optimistic while recognizing that society will have to learn it the "hard way", hitting bottom before trending upward. Realistically, living through the LCN will take more than one generational period and a permanent environment of societal struggle. I often wonder if the US can avoid the LCN downward spiral as it appears that the US has passed its LCN peak.

36. Results Orientation

One of the factors in political divisiveness is the fact that too many people lack the ability to stay focused on a goal. A corollary to this factor is the inability to objectively assess obvious results. These factors are elective and therefore, optional, so one must wonder why people act in this manner. One could hypothesize that the goals on both sides of the divide are different. At this point one enters the realm of conjecture. An example can be drawn on bills proposed in Congress. The right has the goal of tax reform that reduce taxes for the majority of Americans. The left criticizes any element of the bill in an attempt to discredit it, and kill the legislation. This will further lead to loss of political power by denying success produced by the opposing party which could lead to their losing their congressional seats. So the critics either don't know or won't accept what their job is in Congress. If results were focused upon with a common goal in mind, the effects of divisiveness could be significantly reduced. This may be the hardest issue to correct. Elected officials need to do the job they were elected to do but forces for re-election are very strong. Couple this with the fact that the general population often assesses issues with partial facts exacerbated by political bias. Unscrupulous politicians exploit these factors for the purpose of keeping their "seats". Perhaps the general population needs to have a reasonable understanding of issues. There is no excuse in today's world that We the People can't educate ourselves to understand both sides of issues, take responsible positions and let those positions be known to our representatives. The age of the passive electorate is gone.

37. Misuse of Language

Communication is arguably our most important societal asset. One aspect of communication is the use of the English language which is specifically taught in high schools and in most cases, a requirement for graduation. English has a number of words to precisely characterize people, things and actions using nouns and verbs in order to communicate with each other. Nowhere is this more prevalent than in the production of laws. So called “progressives” misuse language more than most and for the most obvious political reasons. Words like “undocumented immigrants” versus “illegal aliens” is an example of watering down a description in order to soften enforcement action, win votes or denounce border supporters. Dramatic words are also used like “Armageddon” when criticizing the 2017 tax plan or “people will die” when describing proposed changes to federally supported Health Care. These are designed by the left to sway support away from making sorely needed changes. The worst thing is that the Left knows this but doesn’t seem to care about causing delays while the very people they represent suffer financial loss due to increased tax and health care costs. Using words like racist, misogynist, homophobe, etc., masks the opportunity for progress if one even attempts to discuss the issues affecting these special interests. This does nothing but cause confusion and division. It also slows down communication, constantly driving for understanding actual meaning instead of concluding debate with real action.

38. Hypocrisy

It used to be "You'll know it when you see it" but these days hypocrisy is cleverly cloaked in satire or faux outrage. It happens on a daily basis but it is hard to know if the voting public in general can "see" it. On a daily basis one can see just how little the voting public knows about finances, free market economy, effects of established socialism/fascism, free speech and personal responsibility. The political left is taking advantage of these low information people, for no other reason but self-service. In the end, We the People are victimized. Problems go unsolved, voter ignorance grows and unscrupulous people end up in power. This is not an anomaly. Half the people in the US actually vote for these deceivers. We may get past the point of no return to our founding values.

39. Accountability

Service providers, including elected officials, are generally held unaccountable. Manufactured product quality has deteriorated without much protest as well. For years campaign promises have been a joke. "Fails" by nearly every kind of service provider are on the rise in an epic way. Restaurant food quality, billing mistakes, feckless prescription drugs, misleading advertising, elected official posturing, failing schools, etc. Why do we consumers tolerate it? In every case, we are victimized by these "fails" and generally do nothing to stand up for ourselves. Get smart folks! We are paying for these services and we are not getting our money's worth. We don't have to tolerate poor quality, anywhere. Speak up! The perpetrators of said fails are not hearing or not bothered by complaints or aware that consumers are going away unsatisfied or just going away. This is what free speech is for. Demand excellence.

The electorate needs to prioritize their voting choices and be responsible voters by knowing the issues and challenging elected officials on their performance. Don't let them get away with excuses for failure.

40. Future of Political Parties

It used to be that one could judge a political candidate by which party supported them. No more. Unless you have been in a cave, you know how fractured and divisive political parties have become. They protect their own, are disgustingly ideological and are focused only on their re-election…. Constituents be damned. The DNC and half our young people have moved so far to the left that they are unrecognizable as US patriots. The Republicans are fractured politically to the point where consensus cannot be achieved. Trump proved that party financial wealth is no indicator of success. Groups like TPUSA and the Tea Party could morph into new "parties" in unique ways with the application of modern technology. There are several inexpensive ways to get information to the general population more effectively. Voters are going to have to spend the time to inform themselves. Life now has evolved into what might be called "open book". The term is feared by students everywhere. Open book tests make the assumption test takers have "all" solution information at their disposal. Without explaining the concept any further, I'll just say this. Voters need to be informed because all required information regarding how a candidate might act if elected is available, but it has to be searched out. This means an effort on the part of voters themselves. Some propose that uninformed voters should just stay home on Election Day.

41. Social Pressure

Paraphrasing a comment from who knows where…if you observe two groups of young people one group largely well behaved and the other raucous and not so well behaved, which behavior grows when the groups get together? I probably don't need to answer that question but will mention that what I have referred to as the "Urban Culture" will likely prevail over "traditional behavior". When it comes to behavior, western culture seems to be moving steadily toward "anything goes". This reveals itself daily in lack of respect for any authority, disturbingly "casual" dress in public, defiant students supported by parents and educators, diminished quality of education, irresponsible news reporting, and self-serving politicians. There appears to be little impetus to move away from these new "norms" until people either see a benefit to do so or are forced to change by negative consequences.

42. Food Stamps, School Meals

Student performance is diminished when students are hungry. They come to school without breakfast and have no lunch from home. This isn't rocket science. It doesn't take a psychologist to know this. Well intentioned people have increased school budgets to fund breakfast and lunch for students in school. The major unintended consequence of this is a dependence culture. The problem is that this issue is being dealt with ineffectively. Let's take the Man from Mars approach instead of the PC approach. Who is supposed to feed and care for school age children? Who is supposed to see that their child is safe from harm? Who is supposed to raise children to be responsible and contributing members of society? Answer to all three questions. … Parents. It is simply not the responsibility of the schools to do the parents' job. Parents should do this for their children but sadly, many do not. It is obvious that schools or government can't motivate parents, so we need to encourage them by enforcing child protective, truancy and education laws.

43. Main Stream Media

In the Founder's historical context, the "press" has been characterized as the people's watchdog. To that end the press has been granted the most broadly protected status for free speech, the 4th Estate is one term describing the press. The US is of course, a free market society and today, the 4th Estate needs to be a viable business that must survive in competition with other communication sources. In colonial times 4th Estate sources were severely limited technologically, often having only one "newspaper". This meant that survival of the newspaper wasn't a problem among competitors, because there were only a few and in some cases, none. The result was that the press was easily able to act ethically and honestly. With so many sources of news today, the news is comprised of several communicative formats and ability to ferret out detailed information resulting in competition among the media. We the People with limited time are totally swamped with information and the 24 hour multisource news cycle. The result of this is sort of leapfrog effect of news stories all with questionable accuracy. What is more alarming is that there is so much information that last hour's news is fogged by the current hours' news which will soon be fogged by next hour's news. This is exacerbated by the fact that too many news watchers are on a constant search for events, the more salacious, the better. Couple this with the increasing lack of education and moral decay, and we have a witch's brew where We the People know everything and know nothing. Too few people live by solid values and understanding, so poor decisions on their own well-being are often made. The conundrum is how can we move our society in a more positive direction and avoid becoming a societal burden. The good news is there are many sources to grasp honest and complete reporting, the bad news is that many people won't seek it out. They display very little "moral compass" and/or have the ability to focus on what is right. Instead they pick a side and stick to the ideological narrative they choose when making important decisions. This make them easy prey for nefarious forces… and they refuse to see it.

44. Scams and Skepticism

These are schemes that can criminally be defined as fraud leading to taking something of value from an unsuspecting person. Scams seem more successful in current culture, probably because people don't see scams as crimes. People used to be able to recognize a scam because they were associated with banking, sales or money transactions so potential scam victims would have their "guards up". Today however, scams appear in political rhetoric, drug culture, school classrooms, online purchases, etc. People don't realize that something of value is taken when these scams are successful. Generally, it is not just money that is the "value" but one's vote, personal information, medical care, family, etc. The point is that we need to take a skeptical stance when dealing with every day interactions, until we can assess motivation or integrity of the "other side". This can slow down communication but that is the point. Slowing down allows time to assess and question motivation. It used to be somewhat obvious when offers were reaching closing date or when demand was supposedly building to the point where one would “miss” a purchase “opportunity”. This happens in different ways for other forms of “value” but taking a skeptical stance and doing some critical thinking will allow for assessment time, leading to better decisions.

45. Sloth by Needy People

Most people are willing to help others who actively try to help themselves. If a person is struggling with job loss, or is hungry or is physically challenged, most people would do the humane thing and help if they can. Conversely, if one takes little action to help themselves, people are less inclined to help. Simple as that may sound, those receiving "help" do not give up so easily. Many entitlement seekers will attempt to embarrass or try to "force" benefactors to support their needs. They claim racism, misogyny, or shame do-gooders into feeling somehow sub-human. Potential benefactors need to have the ability to deny support without accepting the negative claims in order to get needy people to take some observable initiative to help themselves and to stop making poor decisions.

46. Deflecting Responses

Have you ever had, or observed, a debate with a person who keeps changing direction or subjects instead of responding to a debating opponent's point? One can see this quite often during televised debate situations. It seems to happen most often when the debater has a weak or non-factual response that is unable to support their position. The interesting thing is that they don't think others see the deflection and that they form a judgement of the person and the subject. In full disclosure, being a conservative leaning person I have observed deflection happening most of the time by left leaning or activist type people. Some might say that this is a left leaning characterization, but I think the left leaning positions on current issues is weak, and often nonsensical. It is troubling that too many people fall for the weak position, blinded by selfishness, hate or ideology.

47. Elected Officials - Criminality/Defiance

President Trump's election has cause the craziest reactions on the political left. Otherwise intelligent and rational people enter a hate rage when Trump's name or even right leaning people bring up current issues. It seems all logic and respect for opposing views is lost, replaced by extreme rudeness or criminality, even with elected officials. Examples include Oakland Mayor Libby Shaff who warned illegal aliens about impending ICE raids, Jerry Brown signing CA legislation to protect illegal immigrants from ICE, Nancy Pelosi's Armageddon comment regarding the 2018 tax cut and Jobs bill, and calls by Congressional members to "eliminate" ICE.
What planet are these people on and who do they think they are supporting? Let me tell them. We the People…, those that legally elected them.

48. Ideological Barriers (Overton Window)

Ben Shapiro and Dave Rubin posted a discussion on YouTube. They are (or were) two ideological opponents but are able to discuss a broad and controversial number of topics. A "new to me" concept was brought up called the Overton Window (OW). In simple terms it establishes a range of topics that can be logically and unemotionally discussed among those that disagree. Rubin and Shapiro talk about the narrowness of the OW and how it maintains the division of ideologies in the US political arena. Topics that fall outside the OW bring in irrational thoughts and emotions that stifle progress. There are a growing number of people who are beginning to understand the OW and how it can be used to breakdown divisional barriers. Broadening the OW will be a force that can initiate problem solving discussion and action by first focusing on areas of agreement, achieving progress and building on that progress to total solutions. Establishing one's OW can offer a good start for rational debate.

49. Problem Solving Process

There is no sugar coating it. There are proven processes for solving problems. The unfortunate fact is that too few people know what these processes are and how to apply them. The good news is that anyone can understand and apply them. A positive attitude and a healthy intolerance for failure are priceless, don't start without them. Can't do it?... then get out of the way and get someone who can. The hardest part is establishing goal(s), then logically building a plan to solve them, execute the plan and verify results. Knowledgeable and experienced project managers are great sources for improvement process as is the Project Management Institute, the professional association of project managers. Even a healthy dose of openly discussed logic would help to reverse negative debate trends.

50. Ideological Disrespect

Why is it that family members can't discuss religion or politics? In fact, these subjects are regarded by many as taboo for family gatherings. It is true that family dynamics exacerbate disrespect for others' opinions. It seems family members feel they can disrespect each other without the consequences one would expect in a public setting. So, instead of being more respectful in family gatherings, disrespect, even passionate disrespect, has burst into public settings as well.

By what standard does this disrespect have a place in serious debate? We as citizens argue, even violently, among ourselves while we allow, and often re-elect officials who fail to meet their promised obligations while they divergently argue their excuses, then denigrate opposing opinions. It seems obvious that elected officials have forgotten that theirs is a service position that was designed to be temporary and solve problems only they have the elected power to solve. What is worse is that this failure has been tolerated for decades.

Failing politicians are by definition, the swamp, often mentioned… and the swamp's power is being threatened by President Trump and his supporters. It is no wonder the swamp acts irrationally, and therefore should be removed from office. We the People don't need irrational people running our County, State or Country.

Why still, are there so many who argue in support of these failing government actions at the expense of solving the problems? It appears about half of our citizenry shout opposing views down, perform mob behavior, have no solutions and won't even discuss alternatives. I am beginning to accept the idea that Trump Derangement Syndrome is a real psychological condition and anyone with it, should be institutionalized or at least ignored, so the rest of us can work on solving our nation's problems.

APPLIED EPILOGUE

I started this book with Einstein's comment on simplicity. It is important to recognize that simplicity is a relative term, meaning different things to different people. So I am proposing a brief guide. It seems too many people have lost their ability to interact with others in any sort of respectful way. Without going into multiple reasons why so many have devolved into the current ideological quagmire, I'll suggest a simple path to bring us all back to treating each other with respect. This requires one to educate themselves on how to interact with others. We all know, once we can effectively interact, we can solve any problem.

Here are some simple steps to improving your own social interaction and communication. These are listed in increasing levels of complexity, depending on what you need to improve your personal communication skills. Frankly, one shouldn't need to go past the first step. Don't get caught up in what looks like religion, you can do it, it's not that hard. There are many reasons why these concepts have lasted for millennia. Open your mind and/or find other traditional sources. You'll need to look hard for these concepts in today's environment, so let me make it easy for you. Make the effort to understand these ideas and sources, you won't regret it.

1. The Golden Rule: treat others as you want to be treated

2. Win – Win

3. What Would Jesus Do…
   Love God, Love Others as Yourself

4. The 10 Commandments

5. Judeo Christian Principles

6. U.S. Constitution

A few more thoughts…

I've hit the Logic pretty hard in this book but in the interest of improvement, I need to offer a path forward. That is where Leadership comes in. Leadership starts from the inside and shows in one's integrity and ability to focus on goals. That's what leaders do and we all do it in varying degrees. The best leaders have directional sense in almost any situation and act immediately. They are largely unconcerned with criticism because they have confidence in their decisions. Leaders are still just people and unique individuals with their own idiosyncrasies, including what some consider to be a "dark" side. Again to varying degrees, they can appear arrogant or insensitive or singularly focused, and as a human being, sometimes wrong. However, a good leader doesn't quit but changes direction until vindicated by reaching the goal.

We all are required to be leaders. First, for ourselves in choosing a life direction. The moment a person sets life direction, he or she takes on a leader's role. The best of us keep focused on making the most out of life by the actions we take in pursuit of happiness.

Secondly, when placed in a position to lead others either as a parent, a boss or a military commander, it is up to you to continually focus on development, direction or the mission, respectively.

Lastly, be a loyal follower. This does not mean being a blind follower. Adopt the mission expressed by the leader and support him/her in the accomplishment of that mission. Followers should expect clear goals from their leaders. If you can't adopt the mission after serious consideration, remove yourself from the situation to preserve your integrity.

I submit that President Trump is a very good leader and manager. Those in leadership positions should observe President Trump and assess what makes him successful. There is no doubt that he leads the way, stays focused, listens to dissenting opinions, demands performance and produces results. Sure, he aggravates a lot of people but he has enhanced the lives of the majority of the people he was elected to serve. So no one is asked to "like" Mr. Trump personally but we should accept and enjoy the positive results and give him the credit he deserves, because he is doing the job he promised and was elected to do. Leaders should adopt the positive methods he uses and make them their own. Also challenge Trump's actions by digging deeper into his motivation and test them against other leaders and social scientists.

I could go on with leadership as a subject but I promised myself to avoid wordiness in this book. I mention leadership because I think we desperately need more and better leadership, like the rudder on a ship. Hence, the title.

One final thought and challenge… "It's us against them"

There is lots of evidence that our political leaders and a large part of the media have "We the People" politically divided, assumedly for the purpose of maintaining their political and financial power. Let's remember, they work